FRIENDSHIP

FRIENDSHIP

The joy of connection

DR ANTHONY GUNN

hardie grant books

Published in 2018 by Hardie Grant Books,
an imprint of Hardie Grant Publishing

Hardie Grant Books (Melbourne)
Building 1, 658 Church Street
Richmond, Victoria 3121

Hardie Grant Books (London)
5th & 6th Floors
52–54 Southwark Street
London SE1 1UN

hardiegrantbooks.com

A Cataloguing-in-Publication entry is available from the catalogue
of the National Library of Australia at www.nla.gov.au

Friendship
ISBN 978 1 74379 376 3

Cover design by Alissa Dinallo
Typeset in Granjon 11.5/16 pt by Cannon Typesetting
Author photo courtesy of Handprint Photography

Printed in China by 1010 Printing International Limited

To my close friends who I grew up with,
David Rixon, the Fordham boys
(David, Nathan and Trent),
and Shawn Chard.

Small changes make big gains

If someone promised you either $100,000 or
one cent doubled every day for a month, which
would you take? Probably the $100,000, right?
But one cent doubled daily for 31 days would
equal $10.7 million! Our brains tend to look for
the quick fix, but it's small, consistent changes over
time that produce the most gains. As you read
the strategies in this book, focus on making small
daily changes to your social life.

The best thing about the future
is it comes one day at a time.
— Abraham Lincoln

Make friends

Why have friends? Research shows that people with an active social life are healthier, happier and live longer than those who are socially isolated. If you don't have friends, or you haven't been investing enough time in your social life, then this book will give you tips to change this. Make friends! Your life depends on it.

Walking with a friend in the dark is better than walking alone in the light.
— Helen Keller

Choose face-to-face contact

The greatest danger to humans is other humans. This fuels our drive to get along with others and avoid being rejected. It's also why people often prefer to socialise online, behind the safety of a screen. When we remove the natural respect for others that comes with face-to-face interactions, we're more likely to say things we wouldn't normally. Talking to people face-to-face may seem harder than interacting on social media, and a bit uncomfortable, but that's why it's so healthy – it's exercise for our brains. Instead of sending a text or email, pay a visit in person. If this isn't possible, try a phone call. Yes, it's harder, but you'll feel happier. Go on, try it. I dare you!

Two roads diverged in a wood, and I –
I took the one less traveled by,
And that has made all the difference.
– ROBERT FROST

Socialise to feel good

Humans are the most social creatures on the planet. If you want a pick-me-up, socialise. Try chatting to a shop attendant, visiting a friend or family member, or striking up a conversation with someone you don't often speak to, such as a neighbour or a work colleague. Have a short conversation with another person and notice the feel-good endorphins that your body creates. It's a natural high.

To live is the rarest thing in the world.
Most people exist, that is all.
— OSCAR WILDE

Help others instead of yourself

Another way to get an instant hit of endorphins is to help someone in need. Try small things, such as offering directions to someone who appears lost, letting someone go before you in the check-out line, or giving your seat on public transport to someone who needs it more than you. By helping others, you'll also be helping yourself.

When you give yourself,
you receive more than you give.

– Antoine de Saint-Exupery

Practise self-reflection

People become experts in their field by focusing on improving their weaknesses. Novices only focus on their strengths. When it comes to interacting with others, what areas could you improve on? Do you talk more than you listen? Are you pushy with your opinions? Are you too reserved? If you're feeling brave, ask a trusted person for their opinion. Find someone who will give feedback on your behaviours, not you as a person – they need to be constructive, not critical. Looking at our weaknesses can be uncomfortable, but it's the key to rapid improvement.

It's a rare person who wants to hear
what he doesn't want to hear.
– DICK CAVETT

Know your history

From a young age, our loved ones teach us about trust, how to treat – and be treated by – others, and how to make friends. Were you encouraged to speak up about an issue, or to keep quiet and hold a grudge? What about venturing out of your comfort zones, such as going to new places and meeting new people? Whatever your social habits are, it's likely you've learned them from your family. Take time to reflect. Ask yourself what social habits you've been taught and write them down. This simple exercise will help build your awareness about the way you interact with others. Knowing your history will help stop you repeating bad habits.

---

*Those who don't know history
are doomed to repeat it.*
– EDMUND BURKE

Money can buy happiness if spent correctly

It's a common belief that money can't buy happiness. And research does show that, once our everyday living expenses are covered, extra money does little to increase happiness. However, money can increase happiness when it's used to buy experiences, rather than possessions. Research shows that a holiday with loved ones will not only bring longer-lasting happiness than buying a new car, TV or lounge, but will also improve your relationships. This is because holiday memories last, whereas we grow accustomed to possessions. If you can afford to spend a little extra money, choose experiences, not things.

Happiness is determined by factors like your health,
your family relationships and friendships,
and above all by feeling that you are
in control of how you spend your time.
— Daniel Kahneman

Save money

Research shows that it's not necessarily income that makes us happy; it's the amount of money we have saved. People with savings are happier than those without, regardless of their salaries. Money saved is an unconscious confidence booster, guarding against unforeseen events. Seek trusted financial advice and establish a realistic savings budget. Having savings means one less thing to worry about, and the confidence this brings will translate to your social life, allowing you to be more present with those around you.

It's not how much money you make,
but how much money you keep,
how hard it works for you,
and how many generations you keep it for.
— ROBERT KIYOSAKI

Avoid being a bank to your friends

There's an old saying that says if you lend someone $20 and never see that person again, it was probably worth it. Lending money to family and friends is filled with risk for several reasons:

- Paying back the loan is often not a priority.
- It's awkward to ask for your money back.
- Family/social gatherings can become uncomfortable.
- Lending money can actually foster dependence instead of helping the person.
- You might need the money yourself.

Saying no can be awkward, but not as awkward as a loan going bad. Look after your relationships – leave money-lending to the professionals.

Before borrowing money from a friend,
decide which you need most.

– American proverb

Take an interest in others

It's easy to talk, but harder to listen. Many people become anxious when interacting with others because they don't know how to hold a conversation. It's simple: ask questions, and listen to the answers. Instead of trying to teach people about you, focus on them. We can learn something from everyone.

We have two ears and one mouth
so that we can listen
twice as much as we speak.
— Epictetus

Learn three things about a person

Meeting someone new can cause anxiety. Take the focus off yourself by aiming to learn three things about the person you are talking to. For example:

- Where are you from?
- What do you do for work?
- What are you passionate about at the moment?

Make an effort to ask questions when meeting people, and listen to the answers with genuine interest. Watch your likeability increase.

---

*Questions are the breath of life
for a conversation.*
– James Nathan Miller

Maintain eye contact

When people feel socially anxious, they often avoid eye contact. This can make it difficult for them to gauge how well they are interacting. Maintain eye contact with the person you are talking to. Avoid staring at them; break eye contact regularly by slowly blinking or briefly looking away. Practise with a trusted person, or video yourself talking in the mirror. Eye contact, when used correctly, is a valuable asset that helps build rapport. Avoiding eye contact can push people away.

Eye contact is way more intimate
than words will ever be.
— Faraaz Kazi

Make individual eye contact when giving a speech

When giving a speech, your brain identifies three or more people as a crowd. If you were to speak to only one person, the chances are your discomfort would drop. So, if you have to give a speech, pick out individual faces in the crowd and speak directly to them. After a short period, shift your focus to another person, and so on. This tricks the fear centre of our brain into believing we are only talking to one person, which lowers anxiety.

One of the goals I've set myself is to make eye contact
with everyone in the audience at least once.
You can't stop in any one position for too long,
and just that physicality, that need for that,
it's so all-inclusive.
– CHUKWUDI IWUJI

Educate yourself

Try reading up on people and human behaviour. You could read books about body language or dealing with difficult people, or look for guides on ice-breakers to use when meeting new people. The more you know, the more you'll realise you don't know – which is good, because humility lowers other people's defences, making them more comfortable around you.

*An investment in knowledge
pays the best interest.*
– BENJAMIN FRANKLIN

Monitor your speech

How is your choice of words affecting your mental health? Researchers claim that the average person says more than 10,000 words a day. Start listening to yourself. Do you put yourself down, knock back compliments, question your abilities, or even say hurtful things about yourself or others? For one day, try to be fully aware of the things you say. Notice when your words make you feel strong, or weak. Feel the effects in your body. If you want to be strong, say affirming things. It's that simple. Your newfound strength will be reflected in your relationships with others.

You are free to choose,
but you are not free to alter
the consequences of your decisions.
– Ezra Taft Benson

Sleep to socialise

As well as making you feel foggy and irritable, lack of sleep has a string of negative health consequences. People who fall well short of 7–8 hours a night suffer higher rates of heart disease, diabetes, stroke and premature death. They also suffer in the short term, with poorer memory, sex life, health and looks. Make sure your bedroom is conducive to sleep. This includes having a comfortable mattress and pillow, and a well-ventilated room. If noise is an issue, consider wearing earplugs or playing soothing background noise. There are a variety of 'white noise' apps designed for this very purpose. If you are always exhausted, you won't have the energy to socialise.

It is a common experience that a problem difficult at night is resolved in the morning after the committee of sleep has worked on it.

— JOHN STEINBECK

How are your friends influencing you?

The people close to you will influence your daily habits. For example, if none of your friends smoke, you're less likely to smoke. If your friends exercise regularly, you're more likely to be active too.
Take the time to notice how the people you interact with are shaping your life, and how your actions may be shaping theirs.

The people you surround yourself with influence your behaviors, so choose friends who have healthy habits.

— Dan Buettner

Carpool

Sometimes it's easier to travel in a car by yourself. You can listen to the music you like, for starters. But positive social interaction exercises your brain. Engaging with others forces you to think and act in ways you otherwise wouldn't, which in turn forces your brain to grow. Whether it's with colleagues, friends or family, carpooling will not only help the environment by reducing the number of vehicles on the road, it will also benefit your health by forcing you to be social. Who can you organise a carpool with?

Good company in a journey
makes the way seem shorter.
— Izaak Walton

How are you influencing others?

Just as people can unknowingly influence your daily habits, you too can influence theirs. Choose to positively influence those around you. Avoid putting people down or dismissing their ideas. Even if you don't agree with someone's opinion, listen and hear them out. Ask genuinely interested questions. Treat it as a challenge to quietly sit with your discomfort and hear the person out without interrupting them. You might even learn something new. You are influencing others – but are you doing it in a positive or negative way?

Think twice before you speak, because your words and influence will plant the seed of either success or failure in the mind of another.

– NAPOLEON HILL

Assert your boundaries with others

People tend to do whatever you let them get away with. If you feel you're often given more work than others, or that your efforts aren't acknowledged, it's possible that your good nature is being taken advantage of. Saying nothing is setting the standard for how you want to be treated. Whether at work, home or sport, speak up and set boundaries around what you do and don't want. Practise setting firm boundaries in smaller areas of your life – this will build your confidence. Setting clear boundaries is the best defence against feeling used and resentful. What will your new boundaries look like?

Honouring your own boundaries is the clearest message to others to honour them, too.
– GINA GREENLEE

Setting boundaries with difficult people

At times you may come across people who take joy in treating others badly. Whether it's being put down, being asked for non-reciprocal favours, being stood up, or being talked over, be clear about what you're willing to accept. People are usually reluctant to stand up to bullies, and if you do assert yourself, they may simply claim they were only joking. Remain calm and weather the storm – the discomfort won't last long. Once you've set a boundary, this person will likely think twice about using the same tactic on you again.

'No' is a complete sentence.
– Anne Lamott

Know when to walk away

Knowing when to leave an unhealthy friendship is just as important as knowing how to make friends. Far too often, people stay in unhealthy relationships because they fear being alone. But walking away from an unhealthy friendship frees up time and energy, which can then be devoted to nurturing healthy relationships.

It is far better to be alone,
than to be in bad company.
— George Washington

Personal hygiene

Poor personal hygiene can be a significant barrier to making friends. Whether a person has body odour, poor grooming, or habits such as spitting or snorting, your desire to connect and get to know them better will likely be low. Remember, if you feel this way about someone else's personal hygiene, chances are people will feel the same about you. Make sure you are pleasant to be around.

Hygiene is two thirds of health.

— LEBANESE PROVERB

Bad breath

Bad breath, also known as 'halitosis', is a great way to put a strain on a friendship. The problem is, we often can't tell if our own breath smells. Without wanting to cause unnecessary concern, it is worth being mindful of how your breath smells. Food odours, poor oral hygiene, a dry mouth and dental or medical issues are all common causes of bad breath. Being aware of how your breath smells is a form of courtesy to others, and makes it easier for people to remain engaged with you.

Odours have a power of persuasion
stronger than that of words,
appearances, emotions, or will.
— Patrick Süskind

How to spot a fake smile

People-watching can be fun, and it's a great way to distract yourself when feeling self-conscious in public. One thing to focus on is the authenticity of people's smiles. Signs of a fake smile include:

- Only the mouth moves, without the skin around the outer eyes wrinkling.
- A fake smile appears more on one side of the face – often the right side.
- Fake smiles appear faster, and finish faster, too.

But if you do spot a fake smile, don't be too quick to judge. People often fake a smile as a mask to hide behind when feeling unhappy. Start noticing when people fake a smile, or even better, notice when you do it. If you spot a fake smile in a friend, take the time to find out if they're okay.

People may be smiling, but look to the eyes
because they can't hide the sorrow, pain,
and heartache they're trying to hide
behind their smile.

— KARON WADDELL

Good posture promotes a good mood

Our mood often follows our posture. In our society, many people spend long periods of time sitting, which often promotes bad posture. Bad posture can cause a variety of problems, such as neck and back pain, and it also flattens one's mood. Our early ancestors saw bad posture as a sign that a person was sick, and potentially contagious. Even though this is rarely the case today, our primitive brains unconsciously think in a similar way, seeing bad posture in others as a sign to be wary of them.

Good posture will make you feel more confident, and healthier, because your muscles are working together instead of against themselves.

Good posture means keeping your head upright, looking forward, with your back straight and your shoulders pulled back. The positive mood that comes with having good posture will make you more appealing to other people. What is your posture like at the moment?

Good posture is the one most important thing anybody can do now to look better.
— HELEN GURLEY BROWN

Remembering names

The human brain is wired to remember people's faces more easily than their names. When you meet someone new and they tell you their name, repeat it back straight away: 'Nice to meet you, XX …'. Then, during your conversation, make sure you repeat their name at least twice more. This will help you remember it. Try this the next time you meet someone new.

Remember that a person's name is to that person the sweetest and most important sound in any language.

— DALE CARNEGIE

Helping others remember your name

If you find it difficult to remember other people's names, spare a thought for those who forget yours – especially while they are talking to you. If you sense that someone has forgotten your name, help them out by mentioning it in conversation. For example, 'I said to myself, Anthony, I wonder if you'll meet someone you know at this gathering.' Helping others save face when they've forgotten your name will make you more likeable.

Our prime purpose in this life
is to help others.
And if you can't help them,
at least don't hurt them.

– DALAI LAMA

Have an opposite day

Our small, unhelpful habits shape who we are and what we do. Changing small habits allows you to reshape your life. Here is a challenge. For one day, try doing the opposite of what you would normally do. This doesn't mean not going to work – unless you are a workaholic. Examples include: leave a tip if you don't usually do so, take public transport if you usually drive to work, or take a packed lunch from home instead of buying it. Small changes help open your mind to the possibility of bigger changes in your life. What small habit can you do the opposite of?

Quality is not an act,
it is a habit.
– ARISTOTLE

Approach confrontation differently

Some people are excellent at dealing with confrontation, whereas others will suffer in silence for fear of upsetting others. Try approaching confrontation differently. If you are used to standing up for yourself, being so accustomed to confrontation can make you appear aggressive. But avoiding confrontation at all costs can result in isolation. Whether it's asking a friend to slow down when they're driving, asking if you can leave work early, or saying no to a request, try approaching the situation differently to the way you usually would. This will open your eyes to your current habits, allowing you to assess if change is needed.

When you're through changing,
you're through.
– BRUCE BARTON

You can't fix people

Trying to change someone before they're ready to change will only frustrate both you and them. The person has to want to change, and the change they make may not meet your expectations. It can be tempting to surround ourselves with people we think need fixing, as a way of taking our minds off our own problems. This is akin to using others to make ourselves feel good – it often feels good at first, but in the long run will probably lead to conflict and resentment. Instead of trying to fix people to fit your expectations, accept and support them as they are.

Don't walk in front of me; I may not follow.
Don't walk behind me; I may not lead.
Just walk beside me and be my friend.
– ALBERT CAMUS

Goals are a guide, not something to be worshipped

It is important to have goals in life, as they offer direction, but people often feel like they have failed if they don't achieve a particular goal. Life can take us on different paths – often better than we ever expected. The trick is to pursue your goals, but remain open to change. A change in direction may initially be painful, but often results in unexpected happiness. If you remain open to opportunity, you will find it in the most unlikely of places. Treat your goals as a guide, not as a god.

A goal is not always meant to be reached,
it often serves simply as something to aim at.
— BRUCE LEE

Avoid rescuing others from their pain

It's awful when someone close to you is suffering – that's why we often step in to try and fix things. But when it comes to emotional pain, this isn't always the best option. When someone starts describing their troubles, we're often quick to cut them off and reassure them that everything will be fine. But being able to talk through our problems helps our brain process the distressing emotions. Sit with your own discomfort and let the person talk. If you feel you can't offer the best support, perhaps suggest they see a health professional. Be respectful of other people's pain. Sometimes that's the greatest help you can give.

We cannot be more sensitive to pleasure without being more sensitive to pain.
– ALAN WATTS

Make memories

When deciding whether to go out or stay at home, ask yourself which choice is likely to make a lasting memory. Even if you go camping with friends and it rains the whole time, this is more likely to leave a lasting memory than staying at home and watching TV. It's the memories we choose to make that give us the most happiness. Try to make memories that you'll not only look back on fondly, but that will also motivate you to make more.

Memories are the key not to the past,
but to the future.

– Corrie Ten Boom

Conversation starters – slow down

If you get tense when talking to others, the rush of adrenaline caused by anxiety can make you speak too quickly. A simple strategy to combat this is to consciously slow yourself down. Focus on your speed when you walk, eat, breathe and speak. When you mindfully slow down your movements, you are telling your brain that you're not in danger. This will stop the adrenaline rush. Next time you're in a social situation, focus on slowing yourself down. You'll feel yourself relax.

Slow down and enjoy life. It's not only the scenery you miss by going too fast – you also miss the sense of where you are going and why.
– Eddie Cantor

Take up a social hobby

A great way to make new friends and meet new people is to take up a hobby within a group. It may be dancing, choir, craft, book club, using radio-controlled gadgets, hiking, volunteering or sport. Having a common interest makes it easier to make new friends. What hobby could you try?

Find a group of people who challenge and inspire you, spend a lot of time with them, and it will change your life.

– AMY POEHLER

How messy are you?

One barrier that can keep people from having friends over is mess. In extreme cases, such as hoarding, a person will surround themselves with objects as substitutes for relationships with people. It's true, objects can't hurt you like people can – but they can't bring happiness like people can, either. Whether it's your home, your car or your desk, having an orderly environment will make both you and your friends more comfortable. What mess can you tackle?

Clearing the clutter in your physical space
will go a long way toward clearing the clutter
in your mind and your relationships.
– Peter Walsh

Turn social challenges into habits

The relationships in our life give us meaning and happiness. At the end of each day, ask yourself what social contact you have had, and if it has made you grow as a person. Challenge yourself to develop good social habits, such as calling a friend regularly, organising a catch-up with friends, or accepting an invitation. You will need to perform each new action for at least four weeks before it becomes a habit. What social challenge can you start making a habit of?

Watch your thoughts; they become words.
Watch your words; they become actions.
Watch your actions; they become habits.
Watch your habits; they become character.
Watch your character; it becomes your destiny.
– Lao Tzu

Choose arguments with caution

Whether it's discussing politics, religion or any other divisive issue, many people believe that a good debate is healthy. But most people hold a grudge after losing an argument. This is because arguing triggers psychological defence mechanisms, which direct blood flow to the more primitive parts of our brains. There are times when it's important to engage in an argument, such as standing up for yourself, or someone else. But before you engage, ask yourself if it's a fight worth having. If the topic doesn't directly involve you, use caution. Arguing can have its benefits but, as with many other combative endeavours, you'll likely come away upset and hurt – even if you win.

The only way to get the best of
an argument is to avoid it.
– DALE CARNEGIE

Listen to different opinions

A good exercise is to listen to the opinions of people you disagree with. Regardless of the topic, listen to what they have to say. Listening doesn't mean you are agreeing with them. A flexible mind can entertain a range of views. The next time someone brings up a controversial topic, practise listening instead of reacting. This may be challenging, but think of it as bicep curls for your brain – you'll get stronger. You may even learn something new, especially about yourself.

It is the mark of an educated mind
to be able to entertain a thought
without accepting it.

– ARISTOTLE

Socialise for health

People who are more social are healthier, happier and live longer than those who isolate themselves. However, research suggests that people with above-average intelligence enjoy their own company more. The temptation to lock yourself away and work on projects by yourself may be appealing, but it may not be the best option for your health. Think of socialising as exercise for your brain. Often we don't want to exercise, but we usually feel better for it afterwards. Force yourself to socialise and be friendly. You will be happier and healthier for it.

Independence? That's middle class blasphemy.
We are all dependent on one another,
every soul of us on earth.

– GEORGE BERNARD SHAW

Keep a people diary

Our brains are designed to prioritise remembering bad events over good events. Remembering bad events reminds us to avoid these situations, helping us stay safe in the future. This poses a problem in our everyday lives, however, because it means we're more inclined to remember negative social interactions than positive ones, which can fuel our desire to isolate ourselves. A simple trick to combat this is to start keeping a people diary. Record all the positive interactions you have with people each day. Then, if you are ever feeling down and don't want to socialise, read through your diary. It's sure to give you a lift. What memories can you use for your people diary?

I never travel without my diary.
One should always have something
sensational to read in the train.
— OSCAR WILDE

Use humour

Humour, if used correctly, can be a great way to lower people's guards. When we laugh with others it releases feel-good endorphins, and reassures us that the people we are with are not threatening. Read joke books or watch comedians. Quoting a comedian's joke can be safer – if the joke falls flat, you can blame the comedian. Alternatively, poke fun at yourself – just be careful not to go overboard. This shows you're non-threatening and likeable. Try bringing a bit of humour into your social life.

Never be afraid to laugh at yourself, after all, you could be missing out on the joke of the century.
– DAME EDNA EVERAGE

Use curiosity to fight boredom

If you've ever been stuck with someone you find boring at a social function, you'll know how painful it can be. If you find yourself in this situation again, try using curiosity. Be curious about the person; find out as much as you can about them. Alternatively, be curious about your own feelings of boredom. What are you thinking and feeling about the situation? Do certain thoughts make the feeling of boredom better or worse? What about your breathing patterns, or your body language? Be curious and you'll never be bored again.

The cure for boredom is curiosity.
There is no cure for curiosity.
– ELLEN PARR

Let your actions speak loudest

As the saying goes, actions speak louder than words. When telling others about your future plans, avoid talking them up – you'll likely come across as an attention seeker. Besides, if your plans don't come off the way you predicted, you'll lose credibility. Speak less about your intentions, and let your actions speak for you.

Bragging about yourself violates norms of modesty and politeness – and if you were really competent, your work would speak for itself.

— ADAM GRANT

Fight procrastination by informing others

There is an exception to the previous tip. If you have trouble with procrastination, then do tell people what your future plans are. You might intend to join a gym or new group, look for a new job, or organise an event for your friends. The fear of losing face acts as a motivator, encouraging you to follow through on your plans. What future plans are you about to embark on?

The best way to predict the future is to invent it.

– ALAN KAY

Be slow to judge others

Have you ever been let down by someone who failed to deliver on their promise? Whether they turned up late, cut corners or used a worn-out excuse, before assuming that this person did so because they dislike you, pause. Generally, people fail to do what they promised not because they want to hurt you, but because they have inadequacies, such as poor time management or planning skills. They may not be up to the task; this is good to know for future reference. As an old saying states, there's no such thing as perfect people, only perfect intentions. Next time someone lets you down, ask yourself if their behaviour can be better explained by incompetence, rather than malice.

Never attribute to malice that which
is adequately explained by stupidity.
– HANLON'S RAZOR

Do you have anger issues?

Anger issues are almost guaranteed to push people away. Arguments, fractured relationships, fights, damaged property and dangerous driving are common consequences of uncontrolled anger. Anger is a normal emotion, and it's not necessarily bad. It motivates us to respond when there's injustice, such as someone being treated unfairly. But when your anger makes you react blindly, without thinking, it's controlling you. If someone else makes you angry, put yourself in their shoes. Why might they have behaved the way they did? Maybe they lost their job or someone they love, are having trouble with their health, or aren't sleeping properly. Allowing for such possibilities will help keep your own response from being fuelled by anger.

When anger rises, think of the consequences.
— Confucius

Know your triggers

We all get angry at times. Anger is often a defence mechanism against a potential threat – especially the feeling of loss of control. But excessive anger can be a result of lifestyle. Lack of sleep, excessive stress, poor diet, financial or personal issues, or dependence on substances can all be triggers for anger, as they can all signal that a person is not in control of their life. Trying to control anger while ignoring the factors that are triggering it is unlikely to work. If anger is an issue for you, consider which lifestyle factors may be keeping your anger alive?

The need for control always comes
from someone that has lost it.
– SHANNON L ALDER

Respect limits

We are told that winners push the limits, and that we should do the same. But when it comes to social interactions, this doesn't always work. For example, drinking to excess at a work function is unlikely to end well. Similarly, doing all the talking when you meet someone new will likely push that person away. Respecting limits isn't a sign of weakness – it's smart. Whether it's taking turns in a conversation or showing good manners towards others, be respectful of the limits in social interactions. What are the limits in your social interactions?

The difference between stupidity and genius is that genius has its limits.
— ALBERT EINSTEIN

Try skipping the small talk

If you want to be engaging when you meet someone new, step out of your comfort zone by asking interesting questions. Most people will simply talk about the weather, or other safe topics. Small talk does have its place – it helps each person determine if the other is safe to talk to. But breaking normal conventions by asking meaningful questions speeds up rapport building.

For example:

- What has been the best part of your week?
- Besides work, what gets you up in the morning?
- Are you working on any interesting projects at the moment?

Asking significant questions can feel uncomfortable at first, but it can help you get to know the other person much more quickly. Consider asking meaningful questions next time you meet someone new.

I hate having to do small talk. I'd rather talk about deep subjects. I'd rather talk about meditation, or the world, or the trees or animals, than small, inane, you know, banter.

— ELLEN DEGENERES

Are your friendships equal?

When you talk to friends, is the conversation evenly balanced, with equal amounts of listening and talking? If you find yourself doing all of the listening, or all of the talking, it's time to evaluate yourself. If you're always listening, you may need to work on your assertiveness, or reassess the friendship. If you're always the one talking, this may mean you need to work on your listening skills. Examining the way we interact within our friendships can be a good way of highlighting areas we could improve on. How balanced are your friendships?

One of the most beautiful qualities
of true friendship is to understand
and to be understood.

– Lucius Annaeus Seneca

Social media encourages comparisons

We often compare ourselves to others. This is called social comparison. It helps us gain a better understanding of ourselves, and it's vital for learning, because humans learn best by copying others. For example, children learn by copying their parents, and athletes learn technique by copying their coach. But when social comparison is used for determining status, rather than as a tool for learning, it becomes harmful. Are you using social media for positive learning, and to stay in contact with friends and family? Or are you using it to compare yourself to others?

The reason why we struggle with insecurity is because we compare our behind-the-scenes with everyone else's highlight reel.
– STEVEN FURTICK

What are your social media friends costing you?

Spending your time following others' experiences on social media leaves less time for having your own. Hearing about other people's experiences can give us pleasant feelings – this is known as vicarious enjoyment. But these pleasant feelings are no match for our own physical experiences. Watching your friends enjoy overseas holidays, fine food or new purchases may initially be enjoyable, but will likely end in you feeling resentment, or questioning your own choices. Everything in life has a price. Decide which social media friends are bringing you enjoyment and which are costing you, and refine your choices.

When a human being becomes a set of data on a website like Facebook, he or she is reduced. Everything shrinks. Individual character. Friendships. Language. Sensibility.

— ZADIE SMITH

Step away from the screen

The more time we spend on pointless activities, the more likely we are to feel we must be an expert at this activity in order to justify the time spent on it and increase self-esteem. Imagine if you stayed off social media for six months, and instead used your time to visit new places, meet new people and/or do new things. Not only would you be a happier and more interesting person, but your life experience would be deeper. Communicating online to develop social skills is like expecting to get fit by watching sport on television. There's no substitute for the real thing. Turn off the screen, venture outside, say hello to someone new and feel your happiness soar.

*It takes discipline not to let
social media steal your time.*
– ALEXIS OHANIAN

Protect your personal information

It only takes a moment to spill a bag of sugar in the kitchen, but it takes a lot longer to clean it up. Similarly, if your personal information is stolen, it can be very difficult to rectify the problem. It's becoming increasingly common for people to have their personal details stolen online. Investigate ways to protect your information, both by educating yourself about scams and by putting professional safeguards in place, such as online warning systems. When someone has their personal details stolen and used unlawfully, this can result in the person struggling to trust others, which can make it difficult to form new friendships. What safeguards can you put in place to protect your personal information?

The aim of the wise is not to secure pleasure, but to avoid pain.

— Aristotle

Have a 'no tech' day

Communicating with people through electronic devices has been shown to decrease people's face-to-face communication skills. If you are daring, commit to a whole day without looking at an electronic device. You may experience withdrawal symptoms at first, becoming fidgety, annoyed and irritable. Resist the urge to succumb – instead, try doing something physical to take your mind off it. Go for a walk, cook something new, or go on a picnic. Tell family and friends about your 'no tech' day – perhaps some of them will join you. Once you get past the initial discomfort, which won't last long, you'll be amazed and shocked at how much of our lives are consumed by electronic devices.

Technology is a useful servant,
but a dangerous master.
– CHRISTIAN LOUS LANGE

How do you attribute blame?

There's a concept in psychology known as the
fundamental attribution error. Simply put, it
means we blame other people's mistakes on
their personalities, but our own mistakes on our
surroundings. For example, a driver misses a green
traffic light because they are not paying attention.
If it was a driver in front who'd missed the light,
we might say they were rude, lazy or incompetent.
But if we were driving, we'd likely blame it on
being tired, distracted, or a variety of other excuses.
The next time a person makes a mistake, instead
of blaming them personally, stop and ask yourself
what might have contributed to their actions.
How are you attributing blame for mistakes?

*To forgive is to set a prisoner free
and discover that the prisoner was you.*
– LEWIS B SMEDES

Remember a lost loved one

Have you lost someone dear to you? It may have been a family member, a close friend or a pet. The pain associated with grief can be intense, especially when the rest of the world seems to carry on unaffected. This can cause a person to worry that they, too, will forget their loved one. This underlying worry can keep the person from being present when interacting with others.

We all grieve differently. One option is to have a photo of your loved one on display. Each day, put the photo somewhere different. This will keep you from getting used to the photo and reduce the fear of forgetting your loved one.

Happiness is beneficial for the body,
but it is grief that develops
the powers of the mind.
— Marcel Proust

What did you do today to improve your social life?

People often fall into the trap of thinking that one particular achievement will improve their social life. For example, once you have the new car, house, clothes, career or mobile phone, people will like you. But friendships are built on trust, and trust takes time to develop. Instead of trying to impress others with things, impress them by paying attention to them. Phone or visit a friend, just to say hello. Join an interest group, sport or charity, or organise a fun lunchtime event at work. Not every attempt will work, and that's okay. The key is to try several small things. If you plant enough seeds, you will see growth.

Don't judge each day by the harvest you reap but by the seeds that you plant.
– ROBERT LOUIS STEVENSON

Rein in the extremely talkative person

Have you ever been stuck with a person who could talk underwater, trapped by your fear of appearing rude if you cut them short? A number of things can cause a person to talk excessively in social situations, such as anxiety, hyperactivity, or poor social skills. One solution is to steer them towards a topic that interests you. Ask their opinion about a current topic, or ask if they know anyone in a field you want to pursue. You'd be amazed where you can find contacts. Even if the flow of their words is uncontrollable, you may at least be able to direct it. Finding a way to gain something from the conversation will give you a sense of control, instead of feeling like a prisoner to the conversation.

You may not control all the events that happen to you, but you can decide not to be reduced by them.

– MAYA ANGELOU

How to escape the extremely talkative person

There will be times when you simply want to leave the conversation, feeling that everything has been discussed. The trick is to do this without causing offence. One way of doing this is by involving another person in the conversation. Either introduce a friend to this person, or ask the person to introduce you to someone else in the room. Alternatively, excuse yourself by asking if they know where the toilet is, saying you're going to get another drink, or helping someone else with a task, such as collecting dirty plates. Feeling like you're being held hostage in a conversation is not only painful, it can encourage socially avoidant behaviour. Knowing how to control when you start and finish a conversation will increase your confidence to socialise more often.

Control your own destiny or someone else will.
– JACK WELCH

Take a chance

We all have limitations in our lives. These can be determined by our body type, physical health or finances. But there are no limitations on what we can do to improve ourselves. When we step out of our comfort zone, we become more interesting as a person. Try reading a new book, visiting a new location or taking up a new hobby that encourages physical movement. The discomfort we feel when stepping out of our comfort zone is a sign we are growing as a person. What small challenges could you do to try new things that you previously thought were impossible?

Do not go where the path may lead,
go instead where there is no path
and leave a trail.
— RALPH WALDO EMERSON

Live a memorable life

Give meaning to your life by supporting a worthy cause. This may require stepping out of your comfort zone. Push yourself to be your best and your life will take on more meaning. This might mean joining a volunteer environmental group, engaging in an adventurous trek to raise money, or starting/supporting a charity that you feel passionate about. When your life has meaning it will be remembered by others long after you are gone.

The key to immortality is first living a life worth remembering.
— Bruce Lee

Are you supporting bullying?

Do you suffer from a bullying boss, friend or family member? By not standing up to bullies, or laughing along with a bully when they put someone else down, we are unwittingly encouraging the bullying behaviour. Although self-reflection is never easy – it's often painful looking at our imperfections – this is where personal growth can occur. If you're not sure if you've been using bullying behaviour, or encouraging bullying, consider asking a trusted person's opinion. If you want to be respected, you first need to respect others by not encouraging bullying.

My pain may be the reason for somebody's laugh.
But my laugh must never be the reason for
somebody's pain.
– CHARLIE CHAPLIN

Complain with caution

People tend to avoid those who are overly pessimistic and complain a lot. This avoidance is triggered by our primitive brains – for our early ancestors, complaining and being overly pessimistic was often a sign of ill health, which may be contagious. Even though it may feel good to complain about your life, you risk pushing people away. If there are serious issues troubling you, then of course you should talk to a trusted friend or a trained professional. Be selective about who you complain to, and monitor how much of your conversation is taken up with complaints.

Complaining not only ruins everybody else's day, it ruins the complainer's day, too. The more we complain, the more unhappy we get.

– DENNIS PRAGER

Reveal yourself gradually

The layers of an onion are a good analogy for how much to reveal about yourself when meeting someone new. You have to peel away a series of layers before you come to the core. Avoid revealing too much personal information too quickly – doing so will signal a danger alarm, making the other person feel uncomfortable. People should only share personal information with trusted friends, not strangers.

You may feel like you have to reveal all your flaws up-front, otherwise the person will reject you when they find out later on. We all have flaws, so don't feel compelled to declare them up-front.

Be patient about revealing personal information –
instead, talk about less private topics, so the two of
you can build trust and become more comfortable
with one another. Start with the outer layers first –
and resist the urge to cut through too many layers
too quickly, or you risk tears.

---

*Once you've lost your privacy, you realize
you've lost an extremely valuable thing.*
– Billy Graham

How do you rate yourself?

On a scale of 1 to 10, how would you rate yourself as a person overall? Research shows that we are unknowingly attracted to people of a similar self-rating. If we befriend someone with a much higher self-rating, we are likely to feel inadequate, jealous and suspicious, because we believe they will eventually realise they could do better. You might see yourself as dumb because of an unpleasant school experience, or dislike yourself as a result of being teased about your body image or cultural background. Experiences such as these can lead you to hold a lower rating of yourself.

Take the time to honestly rate yourself as a person, then think about the beliefs you hold that contribute to this rating. Are they built on evidence, or are they based on a one-off event or opinion? This can be an uncomfortable exercise, but it's an important step towards realising your full potential.

Low self-esteem is like driving through life with your hand-brake on.
— Maxwell Maltz

Find a successful role model

If you want to be more like the positive, successful and caring people you admire, you need to develop positive attitudes like theirs. Studies show that the easiest way to change our attitudes is to first change our behaviours. Consider the behaviour of people who are popular and respected. What do these people do for work, exercise, friendships, hobbies/interests, self-care, diet, and money management? Investigate by talking to such people, or researching on the internet. We learn best by copying others. Who can you identify as a positive role model? Once you have developed more positive habits, I guarantee your social life will change, too.

Instead of worrying about what people say of you, why not spend time trying to accomplish something they will admire.

— DALE CARNEGIE

Regulate yourself

The body shivers when cold in an attempt to warm itself through physical movement. This only works in the short term, however – the body soon uses up its limited energy supply. We often try to push ourselves in many ways, trusting that our body's energy reserves will see us through. Are you getting enough sleep, enough healthy food, enough exercise, enough rest from work? Are you socialising too much, or not enough? Watching too much TV? We can handle a lot of stressors in small amounts, but when lumped all together, combined stress places considerable strain on our bodies. Instead of expecting your body to keep pushing through, regulate the energy you force it to expend.

Most people spend more time and energy going around problems than in trying to solve them.
– HENRY FORD

Face challenges

There's an old adage that states that if you do what you did, you'll get what you got. Often, our lives are the result of our choices. One of the best choices we can make is to face challenges. If you've set yourself a social challenge, such as attending a new interest group or activity, or going to a fancy dress party, be aware that when it comes time to go, you might try and talk yourself out of it. Discipline is key. Push through your discomfort and follow through on your plan. The discomfort will drop quickly, and the satisfaction of completing the challenge will remain. Choose discipline, and socialise more.

Most people want to avoid pain,
and discipline is usually painful.
– JOHN C MAXWELL

Grudges are toxic

Do you have trouble letting go of a grudge?
Holding a grudge against another person is toxic to
your health. Why? It causes excess release of stress
hormones, which are linked to a variety of health
problems, including heart disease, immune issues
and cancer. If a person's behaviour is harmful,
avoid them. Don't surrender your time and health
by stewing about them. Accept this person for who
they are. Holding a grudge won't change them, it
will only change you – for the worse.

You cannot shake hands
with a clenched fist.
– INDIRA GANDHI

Social anxiety is common

Do you find it difficult to converse with others, feel anxious in public and worry that others are judging you negatively? You may suffer from social anxiety disorder. Research suggests that one in ten adults suffer from social anxiety, and two out of three of those with social anxiety never form an intimate, long-term relationship. Social anxiety can cripple a person's career prospects, relationships and health. If you think this is you, talk to a health professional. Much can be done for social anxiety. Life is too short to live alone. Go on, take the first step: ask for help.

It's not the load that breaks you down,
it's the way you carry it.
— Lou Holtz

Smile, nod, agree

If you get anxious when meeting new people, there are three simple things you can do to increase your likeability: smile often, give small, regular nods of your head, and say that you agree with the person whenever that's the case, reinforcing your agreeable body language. People who are agreeable are seen as more likeable and trustworthy. Remember, keep these three agreeable mannerisms as natural as possible, or you'll risk appearing insincere. Practise being agreeable when meeting new people and watch how they respond.

Since there is nothing so well worth having as friends, never lose a chance to make them.
— FRANCESCO GUICCIARDINI

Have a 'friends' criteria

Our friends can have a large impact on our ability to socialise. We often have selection criteria for choosing cars, homes, clothes, movies and food, but we rarely think about having criteria for choosing our friends. How do your friends treat you? Are they supportive, or do they put you down? Do they share conversations evenly, or dominate? Do they offer help when you need it, or only appear when they want something? Write a realistic list of the things you regard as important in a friendship, then see if your friends come close to meeting these criteria. If they do, congratulations. If they don't, it may be time to consider finding some new friends.

My best friend is the one who brings out the best in me.
– HENRY FORD

Have a 'partner' criteria

Choosing a loving partner is one of the most important decisions we can make. If you are single and looking for a partner, what should you look for? Humans learn to lie as early as three years of age, and we adults are masters at hiding our true intentions. Instead of listening to a person say all the right things, pay attention to their actions. How do they treat their family members, the opposite sex, or people in positions of higher or lower authority to themselves? Are they angered easily? Do they hold a grudge? How do they treat animals? Know what you want before entering a relationship, because love can be blinding. Pay attention to actions instead of words.

Never have a companion that
casts you in the shade.

— Baltasar Gracian

The relationship warning sign

Sometimes it can be difficult to know if a
friendship or relationship is unhealthy or if you're
just going through a rough patch. There is one
simple test, though: If anyone ever blames you
for their bad behaviour, run! This is a strong
indicator of emotional abuse – bad behaviour is
the sole responsibility of the person committing it.
Having a relationship with a person who blames
you for their bad behaviour is likely to lower your
self-confidence and cause you pain. Protect your
mental health by guarding against people who will
emotionally abuse you. Are you being blamed for
others' bad behaviour?

*A healthy relationship will never require you to
sacrifice your friends, your dreams, or your dignity.*
— MANDY HALE

Learn about a different culture

Did you know that black cats are considered bad luck in America, but good luck in Japan? A great way to expand both your mind and your social skills is to learn about another culture. Whether it's food, entertainment, fashion or social cues, we often prefer to conform with what the majority of those in our society deem as normal. Learn about the food, language, transport and customs of another country. Being open to alternative options creates mental flexibility, which is vital for developing good social skills. Which culture could you learn about?

Travel and change of place impart new vigor to the mind.
— Lucius Annaeus Seneca

Dealing with guilt

Do you often feel guilty? Children start feeling guilt as early as three years of age. Guilt involves negatively judging yourself over a specific behaviour. For example, *I forgot their name*, *I should have invited the neighbours*, or *I shouldn't have said what I did*. Negative emotions, such as guilt, occur in the fear centre of the brain, and are generally devoid of logic and rationality.

If you are prone to feeling guilt, it's important to challenge this. If your guilt is warranted, how can you make amends? Often a simple apology fixes things. Bring your guilt out into the open by writing down your concerns or talking with a trusted person. This will engage the logical part of your brain, helping you determine if there is a genuine problem. If that's the case, you can focus on finding a solution. There is always something that can be done. What can you do to start taming your guilt?

Guilt is perhaps the most painful companion of death.
— Elisabeth Kübler-Ross

Dealing with shame

Shame develops around 15 months of age, and can be caused by feeling worthless or defective. Shame often makes a person isolate themselves. Things that can trigger shame may include surviving a traumatic situation when those around you were less fortunate, engaging in an act that you now regret, or winning at someone else's expense. Examine the reasons for the way you feel. Did you genuinely mean to do what you did, or was there another cause? Finally, confess. Tell a trusted person, such as a friend or health professional, about the event that has shamed you. Sharing a problem can help take the weight off your shoulders. If you suffer from shame, what can you do to fix it? Talk to someone – your social life depends on it.

When we hold secrets it creates shame, and shame is a great barrier to success. When you carry the shame you do not allow yourself to fulfill your greatest potential, you do not honour the truth of yourself, you do not honour your highest self. When you let go of the secret, only then you live to your greatest potential.

— OPRAH WINFREY

Look for a positive adrenaline rush

Engaging in an activity that gives you an adrenaline rush can lift you out of feeling that life is mundane. To be a positive experience, the activity causing the adrenaline rush must be one of your choosing, and something you feel a degree of control over. Choose an activity that's challenging for you. This will vary from person to person, but examples might include bungee jumping or sky-diving. For those who are more risk averse, singing karaoke or swimming in cold water might work. Just remember: safety first. What adrenaline-inducing activity have you always wanted to do? Go for it! You'll have a great story to tell.

It is the greatest shot of adrenaline to be doing what you have wanted to do so badly. You almost feel like you could fly without the plane.

— CHARLES LINDBERGH

Reduce cortisol in your life

Ongoing, long-term stress can not only reduce your willingness to meet new people, it can also damage your body. The same adrenal glands that produce adrenaline also produce the stress hormone, called cortisol. When produced in excess, cortisol suppresses immunity, impairs memory, shrinks brain cells and increases weight gain. Work pressures, financial concerns, relationship issues or health worries can all cause excessive stress. If you are having trouble making friends, consider whether you have excessive stress in your life. Excess cortisol may be a factor impacting your ability to connect with others. How can you start reducing the stress in your life?

No good comes from hurrying.

— YIDDISH PROVERB

Burn off cortisol with social exercise

A simple way to reduce stress and cortisol is through exercise. Exercising with others is even better. Not only will you get the benefits of exercise, you'll also get the benefits of socialising. Great ways to exercise with others could include walking with friends (especially at work during lunch, or with other parents if you are part of a parents' group), doing a yoga class, being part of a social group, such as a hiking group, or joining a sporting team. What type of social exercise could you start doing?

Remember, teamwork begins by building trust.
And the only way to do that is to overcome
our need for invulnerability.

– Patrick Lencioni

Embrace imperfection in people

Research shows that models who have a freckle or
irregularity on their face are far more memorable
than those whose image has been perfectly
airbrushed. This is because the brain looks for
unique characteristics to help it remember a person.
Without anything unique to focus on, the brain
falters. This is further evidence that perfection
in people isn't normal. Expecting people, friends
or family to be perfect will only set you up for
disappointment. Only wanting a partner or friends
who have a certain body shape, dress a certain
way or earn a particular level of income will
dramatically limit your social options, and threaten
the authenticity of your friends

Have no fear of perfection –
you'll never reach it.
– SALVADOR DALÍ

Do you have trust issues?

Past trauma can make it difficult to make new friends. If you've been let down, abused, neglected, cheated on or had a crime committed against you, it can be difficult to trust other people. Trust is fragile – once it has been broken, it can be challenging to allow yourself to trust again. But if you keep a wall up to protect yourself from getting hurt again, you'll also be very lonely. Do you have trust issues? If so, are they negatively impacting your ability to interact with others?

It is an equal failing to trust everybody,
and to trust nobody.

– English proverb

Healing trust issues

If you have trust issues, what can you do? First, identify the areas where you struggle to trust others, such as in romantic relationships or being wary of authority figures. Then determine how your trust issues influence your behaviour. Do you become defensive around certain people, or do you become submissive to avoid conflict? Find safe situations where you can practise lowering your guard, such as at a small get-together with close friends or family.

You don't have to lower your guard completely, nor do you have to trust people who have previously let you down. But aim to lower it a little, and notice the increase in the quality of your social interactions.

The best way to find out if you can trust somebody is to trust them.

– Ernest Hemingway

Politely smile at peer pressure

Research suggests that children as young as two show signs of being influenced by peer pressure, and it appears to take full effect around the age of nine. Our tendency to conform may have an evolutionary benefit – accepting the actions of those around them helped our ancestors learn new skills and avoid dangers. Peer pressure isn't limited to teenagers; it affects adults as well.

If you have tried to resist eating chocolate at work or drinking alcohol at a party, but failed due to the encouragement of those around you, then you've experienced peer pressure.

We naturally want to be part of a team, and saying no to the team's request can initially be painful. Just be polite and stand your ground, saying no with a smile. Avoid being confrontational, and just keep repeating the same response. Politely say no to peer pressure – you'll be held in higher regard by those around you.

Freedom is from within.

– FRANK LLOYD WRIGHT

How do you see yourself?

Often our brains lead us to believe untruths about ourselves that negatively affect the quality of our social interactions. Try this small test – tick the appropriate answer.

I'm a bad person	☐ YES	☐ NO
I'm dumb	☐ YES	☐ NO
I'm unlovable	☐ YES	☐ NO
I'm a flawed person	☐ YES	☐ NO

If you've answered yes to any of the above questions, determine if your answer is based on fact or opinion. Remember, an opinion may not be supported by evidence, whereas a fact must be. Do you have proof, or is it just an opinion?

Your visions will become clear only when you can look into your own heart. Who looks outside, dreams; who looks inside, awakes.

– CG JUNG

Question your opinion of yourself

When being critical of ourselves, we often fall into the trap of criticising our self-worth, which lowers our self-esteem and self-belief. If you want to be critical of yourself, then criticise your behaviour, as this can be changed. If you answered yes to any of the previous questions, replace them with the following statements that address behaviour.

I'm a bad person	REPLACE WITH	I have made bad decisions
I'm dumb	REPLACE WITH	I will benefit from further education
I'm unlovable	REPLACE WITH	I act guarded around others
I'm a flawed person	REPLACE WITH	I engage in unhelpful habits

If you do not conquer self,
you will be conquered by self.
– NAPOLEON HILL

Have a candlelit meal with others

Next time you have a meal with friends or family, even if it's just take-away food, sit at the table with candles lit, and turn the lights off. You may all laugh at first, due to the novelty, but the darkness will cut out visual distractions and force everyone to be more focused on each other. You'll be amazed at how it brings you closer together. Go on, try it.

You learn a lot about someone
when you share a meal together.
– ANTHONY BOURDAIN

Stand up for your posture

Sitting for too long not only promotes bad posture, it has also been shown to increase the risk of cancer and ageing, and decrease a person's life expectancy. The good news is that simply standing can help reverse this, and improve posture. If your job requires you to sit for large amounts of time, consider having your printer on the other side of the room, using a toilet that is further away, taking the stairs instead of the elevator, or having a standing desk. The importance of moving around is also another reason to get outside and meet people, instead of sitting at home. Stand up. Your life depends on it.

A good stance and posture reflect
a proper state of mind.
– Morihei Ueshiba

Reinvent yourself

We often fall into the trap of thinking we can only have one type of career, drive one type of car, live in a particular area, or be limited to certain activities. This is usually because alternatives don't fit the mental image we have of ourselves. But this self-image can be changed at any time. Yes, those close to you may initially question your changes, but they will probably get used to them much more quickly than you do. Are you willing to reinvent yourself, one small step at a time?

Life isn't about finding yourself.
Life is about creating yourself.
— GEORGE BERNARD SHAW

Try the small self-change experiment

Often, we will be reluctant to reinvent ourselves for fear of what others will say, especially those close to us. But psychological experiments have shown time and again that people find it hard to detect small changes in their environment. Try this experiment: make a small change to yourself, such as using a new word in a conversation, and see how many people notice. Making small changes over time is a great way to experiment with the temporary discomfort that comes from reinventing yourself.

People become attached to their burdens
sometimes more than the burdens are
attached to them.

– GEORGE BERNARD SHAW

Learn a magic trick

Magic is a great icebreaker and speeds up the process of building rapport. If you don't see yourself as a magician, that's all the more reason to take the time to reinvent yourself, and learn one magic trick. It may be a simple card trick, or you might try making an object disappear. There is excellent instructional information on the internet. Learning magic is a great investment in building and strengthening your social ties. What magic trick can you learn?

*It's still magic even if
you know how it's done.*
— TERRY PRATCHETT

Who are your true friends?

Sadly, a good gauge of who your true friends are is how they respond in times of trouble. Whether it's chronic illness, a mental health diagnosis, the death of a loved one or long-term unemployment, fair weather friends are likely to fall silent, whereas true friends are more likely to stay and offer support. True friends are rare, so make sure you look after them. Who are your true friends, and what are you doing to acknowledge their friendship?

Friends show their love in times of trouble, not in happiness.

— EURIPIDES

Nothing changes if nothing changes

We frequently fall into the trap of making future declarations that we never follow through on. How often have you said to friends that you'll have to catch up, or that you must have them over for dinner, but never do? If you want change in your life, make that change happen. What offers have you made and not fulfilled? Which friend can you catch up with? Go on, do it.

Be the change that you wish to see in the world.

— MAHATMA GANDHI

Openly acknowledge another person's efforts

Have you ever had someone steal your idea, or take credit for something you did? It hurts, doesn't it? People love to be acknowledged for their efforts. Take the time to acknowledge the efforts of someone who has done something to help you. The person may have helped you with a project, taken an appropriate initiative, or offered wise advice during a time of need. If acknowledging their efforts in public, avoid going over the top to prevent embarrassing the person. A simple acknowledgment of the effort they put in and why it was helpful will be enough. Who can you publicly acknowledge for their efforts?

If I have seen further than others,
it is by standing on the shoulders of giants.
— ISAAC NEWTON

Meet your neighbours

Modern technology has allowed us to get to know people on the other side of the world, but, somewhat ironically, many of us don't know our own neighbours. Knowing your neighbours is a great way to build community, and strong communities are often safer communities, as people are more likely to look out for each other. Take the time to get to know your neighbours. It's reassuring to have someone nearby who can offer assistance if needed. You don't need to live in each other's pockets, though – a simple wave can help improve neighbourly relations. Instead of pretending you're busy or heading inside when the neighbours come out, fight the urge and say hello.

Love your neighbor as yourself;
but don't take down the fence.
— CARL SANDBURG

What example are you setting for others?

Whether we like it or not, the way we live our lives acts as a guide for others. For example, if a person eats poorly, doesn't exercise, wastes money on pointless things and socialises with destructive people, or doesn't socialise at all, then this person's life will likely set a negative example. Alternatively, if a person eats well, exercises regularly, uses their money wisely and socialises regularly with supportive people, then their life will likely be a positive example to others. Are you the negative and grumpy type who always finds problems with the world? Or are you optimistic, happy and looking for the next challenge to conquer? Either way, you are acting as an example for others. What example are you setting?

You have to be brave with your life
so that others can be brave with theirs.
— KATHERINE CENTER

Are you always the life of the party?

Sometimes people who are the life of the party actually suffer from social anxiety – being overly extroverted is simply an attempt to hide their discomfort. These people often dread going into social situations because there is an expectation that they will be entertaining. This becomes draining, sometimes causing the person to avoid social situations. If this is you, practise regulating your energy when around others. Resist the urge to be overly loud; instead focus on individual conversations and being authentic. This will feel uncomfortable at first, especially if people comment about your new, quieter manner. However, people will likely adapt to the new you much more quickly than you expect. Be yourself – it's less work.

Nothing so much prevents our being natural
as the desire to seem so.

– François de La Rochefoucauld

Give someone a smile

Smiling releases feel-good endorphins, which help lower cortisol – even if it's a forced smile. Smiling also makes you appear less threatening, and more approachable. Just like yawning, smiling has been shown to be contagious. If someone gives you a non-threatening smile, you'll probably smile in return. Start smiling at others. Try it at work, or if you do the school pick-up, smile at another parent. Smile if you see someone you know in public. If you're guarded about smiling at others for fear you'll get stuck talking, this may signal an issue with setting appropriate boundaries. As long as you are polite, you can leave a conversation whenever you like. Make it your challenge today to smile at someone. You might just change their day.

Try to be a rainbow in someone's cloud.
– MAYA ANGELOU

Are you taking friendships for granted?

Habituation is the term used to describe our ability to get used to things. For example, eat enough chocolate in one go and your enjoyment of the taste will diminish. A similar thing happens with friendships. We can get used to a person and take them for granted, assuming they will always be there. To guard against habituation, write down at least three things you are grateful for about a particular friendship in your life. Reminding ourselves helps stave off habituation. Write your list now, before turning the page.

Even the most caring people can get tired of being taken for granted.

— NISHAN PANWAR

Are you too dependent on others?

The opposite of taking a friendship for granted is being too dependent. This can push people away. A sure sign of being too needy is when a person is taking more from the friendship than they are giving. Do you tend to dominate conversations? Do you avoid doing things by yourself? This can be a sign that you can't cope with your own company. Try spending short periods of time doing things by yourself. Go to the movies alone, or stay home and read a book. If you are comfortable with your own company, people will find you more fun to be around, because you are socialising for fun instead of for dependency.

If you are not happy being single,
you will never be happy in a relationship.
Get your own life first, then share it.

— AUTHOR UNKNOWN

Embrace and face an embarrassing event

Did you do something embarrassing in the past that still makes you cringe when you think of it? Maybe it was tripping over in the rain, having your credit card declined while shopping, inadvertently disclosing a secret to the wrong person, or saying something embarrassing while with a group of friends. Repeatedly going over the experience in your mind is called rumination – this is the brain's attempt to solve the problem.

The more you engage in rumination, the worse the embarrassing event will seem. Instead, tell yourself, 'I cannot change the past'. People will long have forgotten. If you still avoid certain social situations because of this incident, start visiting these places again. It will be challenging at first, but you'll be amazed at how your brain reprocesses the event so it's no longer distressing. What embarrassing event can you embrace and face?

Success is not final, failure is not fatal:
it is the courage to continue that counts.
— WINSTON CHURCHILL

When to have difficult conversations?

We often avoid telling a friend something they don't want to hear for fear it will end the friendship. Whether it's that they have bad breath, are dating a questionable person, or are about to make a bad decision, deciding whether to say something can be agonising. A simple question to ask yourself is: *What will my friend think if they discover that I knew the truth, but kept quiet?*

If saying nothing won't matter, there's a good chance that the issue is simply clashing with your sense of taste. However, if keeping quiet could negatively impact the friendship, that suggests the issue is more pressing, and potentially relates to your friend's safety or wellbeing. If that's the case, rehearse what you want to say, pick the right moment and gently explain why you feel the need to raise this with them. True friends ignore another's imperfections – until those imperfections threaten their safety.

A true friend never gets in your way
unless you happen to be going down.
– ARNOLD H GLASOW

Look after your future self

If you're feeling indecisive about socialising, it can help to ask what impact your decision will have on your future self. For example, you've been invited to a social function, but on the day, you are feeling reluctant to go. If you stay at home you'll probably watch TV and remain feeling unmotivated, and your life will remain unchanged. If you go to the party you may meet someone new. That person could change the direction of your life – they might suggest a new career path or hobby, or offer to introduce you to an important person. It's the people we meet who will have the most influence on the direction of our lives. The next time you're having second thoughts about socialising, think of your future self.

*It is our choices ... that show what we
truly are, far more than our abilities.*
– JK Rowling

Do a good deed

If you want an instant rush of feel-good endorphins, help someone in need. This might mean holding the door of an elevator, giving change to a homeless person, letting someone go first, either at the check-out or in traffic, donating blood, or writing a thank-you note to someone who won't expect it. What good deed can you do for someone?

How far that little candle throws his beams!
So shines a good deed in a weary world.
— WILLIAM SHAKESPEARE

Volunteer

Volunteering your time to help others has been shown to offer a variety of psychological benefits, including: improving your skills in a particular area, helping you pursue new pathways in life, feeling more grateful for your own life, increasing your happiness levels and, most importantly, offering a simple way to socialise more. The quality of our social connections is a strong determinant of our happiness, and volunteering offers a simple way to help achieve this. What volunteer options are available in your area?

Life's most persistent and urgent question is,
'What are you doing for others?'
– Martin Luther King, Jr.

Notice the best in others

Our early ancestors evolved to be suspicious of those outside their tribe or clan. This protective factor kept our primitive ancestors safe, but although it is no longer needed, our suspiciousness remains. This is why gossip magazines, reality TV shows and other media that negatively judge people are so popular. Break this outdated evolutionary trait by noticing the good in those around you. Whether it's work colleagues, friends or family, remind yourself of these individuals' good points. You'll be amazed at the impact it has on remaining positive.

When we seek to discover the best in others,
we somehow bring out the best in ourselves.
— William Arthur Ward

Dare to leave your tribe

Have you noticed that at social gatherings such as parties, weddings or work functions, people tend to gather with those they already know? This is because humans are naturally anxious about meeting new people. Break the evolutionary mould – step out of your perceived tribe or clan, and talk to someone new. Yes, it will take courage. The primitive part of your brain believes that leaving the safety of your tribe and socialising with others is a threat. But it will be worth it. Not only will you get to meet new people, others from your safe group will probably follow, because you've shown it's not dangerous. At your next social gathering, make it your mission to leave your safe group of people and mix with others.

It's not because things are difficult that we dare not venture. It's because we dare not venture that they are difficult.

— Lucius Annaeus Seneca

Notice when your brain worries about the future

Have you ever been seriously anxious before going to a social gathering, such as attending a party or work function, or joining a new group, only to discover that the anticipation was far worse than the actual event? Our brains naturally overestimate risk and underestimate our ability to cope. This was vital for our early ancestors when they were living in caves, but it isn't needed the same way today. To be anxious, our brain must be thinking about the future. When our brain is in the present moment, anxiety is reduced or disappears. Simply being aware of the direction your mind is going in is the first step in being able to control anxious thinking.

*A day of worry is more exhausting
than a day of work.*

– JOHN LUBBOCK

Use mindfulness against anxious thinking

Mindfulness is a form of meditation that trains you to live in the present moment. The key to mindfulness is noticing all aspects of whatever you are doing. If you are walking, how do your feet feel with each step? If you are eating, what does each mouthful taste and feel like? The goal of mindfulness is to break the automatic cycle of unhelpful, unconscious thinking and focus your mind on the present. The instant you become aware of your thinking, you win. Great tasks to promote mindfulness include deep breathing, yoga, exercise, colouring in, and being in nature. When you notice yourself worrying about the future, use mindfulness to calm your thoughts.

If you want to conquer the anxiety of life, live in the moment, live in the breath.

– AMIT RAY

Sugar is the new drug

Research suggests that refined sugar is eight times more addictive than cocaine. Sugar not only leads to weight gain, but also to feelings of drowsiness, fatigue and irritability. Consuming sugar gives us an instant high, which is quickly followed by an instant low. This rollercoaster ride can be disastrous for our motivation levels, which in turn can affect our social lives. Once the sugar low hits, your willingness to interact with others will likely wane. This is why it's so important to cut back on sugary foods and eat healthy where possible. The quality of your social interactions will be affected by what you eat. Fight temptation and reduce your sugar – you'll notice the change in your people skills.

The road to success is dotted with
many tempting parking spaces.
– WILL ROGERS

Compromise in your relationships

Psychologists estimate that in healthy marriages, approximately 30 per cent of problems are resolvable, 50–60 per cent are modifiable, and 10–20 per cent need to be accepted and coped with. In any healthy marriage or friendship, you will have disagreements at times. The majority of these can be resolved through compromise. Look for areas where you can both compromise so neither feels like they're missing out. If you can't compromise on an issue, but you value the relationship, can you accept the situation and move on? Being able to compromise without jeopardising your own needs is crucial for a healthy friendship. What areas can you compromise on when it comes to your relationships?

A tree that is unbending is easily broken.
– Lao Tzu

Check your facts before judging others

It's often difficult to see the positives in people we've already judged negatively. We believe we are experts at judging others, but the problem is, we only remember the times we were right, not the times we got it wrong. For example, imagine a work colleague got extremely drunk at last year's work party, and now you refuse to get to know them, despite the fact that they've attended other work functions and stayed perfectly sober. Psychologists call this the confirmation bias — we pay attention to facts that reinforce our beliefs and ignore the ones that don't.

Have you formed a negative opinion of someone based on limited facts or gossip? If so, your negative judgement about this person may need to be re-examined. Where possible, try this experiment: be nice to this person, and look for facts that contradict your negative opinion of them. It's a small risk that could offer big rewards.

---

*Do you want to be right
or do you want to be happy?*

– Dr Phil

Do you have designer friends?

Some people choose or reject friends on the basis of social status. Becoming friends with a certain person to appear more socially important, or avoiding a friend because they will lower one's social status, is not good for mental health. Why? Because the friendship isn't genuine, meaning you can't rely on it. Secure and supportive friendships are not only the key to happiness, but also to health and living longer.

If you've been choosing designer friends solely because they'll make you look good, keep in mind that, like any fashion, eventually the friendship will go out of style. Alternatively, if a friend ignores you in certain situations, or leaves you to speak to people they deem more important, it may be time to re-evaluate the friendship. Make sure your close friendships are built on authenticity.

False friends are like our shadow, keeping close to us while we walk in the sunshine, but leaving us the instant we cross into the shade.

— CHRISTIAN NESTELL BOVEE

Pause before gossiping

It can be fun to gossip about others – having a common enemy is one of the fastest ways to build rapport with another person. It's also one of the easiest ways to ruin your reputation, because there's no guarantee the person you gossiped with won't talk behind your back. Before you send a message disrespecting someone you know, ask yourself how you'd feel if that person read the message. Once the message is sent, it's out there forever, and the offended person can keep re-reading it, fuelling their anger towards you. Next time you want to send gossip, pause and sleep on it. You may save yourself a lot of unneeded pain.

Great minds discuss ideas; average minds discuss events; small minds discuss people.
– ELEANOR ROOSEVELT

Remember friends' and family's birthdays

Did you know that in a group of 57 people, there's a 99 per cent chance that two of them will share the same birthday? Our birthdays can be one of the most important days of the year. If you want to make someone feel special, remember their birthday. Send a card or a message or, even better, phone them and wish them a happy birthday. Such a simple gesture is sure to have a positive impact.

There are two great days in a person's life –
the day we are born
and the day we discover why.
– WILLIAM BARCLAY

Different friends for different situations

It's normal to have different friends in different areas of your life, as common interests can form the basis of great friendships. For example, you may enjoy a friend's company while playing a sport or talking about an interest such as gardening, even though you may have little in common outside of this. You don't have to dismiss the friend just because you don't have enough common interests. Instead, aim to have friends in a variety of areas. A common trap people fall into is wanting to be friends with people just like them. This is impossible – we are unique! Look to have friends that you can share experiences with, instead of just points of view.

*Friendship is born at that moment
when one person says to another:
What! You too? I thought I was the only one.*
– CS Lewis

Dare to be yourself

Daring to be original is scary, because it means exposing ourselves to scrutiny, judgement and possible ridicule. Playing it safe and blending in with the crowd may seem safer, but it also offers boredom, complacency, and the prospect of never meeting your full potential. That's terrifying! Trust your intuition and start getting to know the real you. What are your tastes, style and personality? If you've been pretending to live a life that's not you, how can you start being yourself? Make small changes to better express who you really are. Maybe it's listening to a new type of music, going to the theatre if you don't usually, or wearing a different style of shoe. Starting today, what small change can you make? Dare to be yourself!

Your time is limited, so don't waste it living someone else's life.
– STEVE JOBS

Follow up an old friendship

Do you have a good friend you've known for a long time, but haven't heard from lately? We are all guilty of intending to follow up with long-lost friends, but not getting around to it. The person may be someone you went to school with, grew up with or shared a significant experience with. Track down their contact details and get in touch. Push through the urge to procrastinate. Life is too short, make contact today. It's sure to bring a smile to your face – and theirs.

It takes a long time
to grow an old friend.
– JOHN LEONARD

Silence may not mean rejection

You may have tried contacting a friend, but
they're taking longer than usual to reply to your
communication. Don't jump to the conclusion that
their silence means rejection or disapproval – this
assumption often proves to be false. Check to see
if your friend is okay. They may be going through
a difficult time, their contact details may have
changed, or they may simply be extremely busy.
Fight the feeling of rejection and replace it with
curiosity, and find out why they haven't replied.

Concern should drive us into action,
not into a depression.
– KAREN HORNEY

Help a troubled friend

Have you been in a situation where a friend has acted out of character? Maybe they were quiet and withdrawn, or bad tempered and irritable, and you didn't know why? Avoid tip-toeing around the subject, and politely ask them if something is wrong. They'll probably be relieved that you asked. If there is an issue, such as a health, financial or emotional concern, work out what you can do to help. It may be as simple as listening to their concerns, or linking them in with a professional who is trained to help in such matters. Help your friend if they need it.

When a friend is in trouble, don't annoy him by asking if there is anything you can do. Think up something appropriate and do it.
— EDGAR HOWE

Friends and business often don't mix

It's natural to want to include friends in new business opportunities, but if you have come up with a great business idea or investment strategy, pause before inviting friends and family to get involved. Many a friendship has been destroyed by a bad business deal. Yes, it can work on some occasions, but it's usually best to look elsewhere for business partners. Protect your friendships by thinking carefully before going into business with a friend.

A friendship founded on business is better than a business founded on friendship.

— JOHN D ROCKEFELLER

Keep a running 'ta-da' list of social achievements

When facing new social challenges, keeping track of your wins will motivate you to keep pushing yourself. You visited friends instead of staying at home? Write it down. You phoned someone instead of texting? Write it down. When meeting someone new you repeated their name at least three times? Write it down. Reflect back on your list regularly to maintain motivation. What social win can you achieve today to add to your list?

Nothing builds self-esteem and self-confidence like accomplishment.
— Thomas Carlyle

Beware of the bystander effect

It's human nature to stand back and wait for others to act, especially during a crisis. This is known as the bystander effect. When a large number of people are present in a crisis, you're less likely to help. Individuals monitor the behaviour of those around them, instead of leading the way. Whether it's seeing a person lying unconscious in a busy street or hearing a smoke alarm go off in a crowded building, you will likely do nothing and wait for someone else to respond. People have lost their lives due to the bystander effect. In a crisis, no matter how small, ignore your initial discomfort and lead instead of standing back. If you act first, people will follow you.

*A leader is one who knows the way,
goes the way, and shows the way.*
– JOHN C MAXWELL

Acknowledgements

Jonathan Dyer, thanks for helping me create
another book; Mel, my wife and the silent second
author of this book, and my children, Emma and
Patrick; my agent Sally Bird; Pam Brewster and
the team from Hardie Grant Books, for giving
me another opportunity; my editors Anna Collett
and Vanessa Lanaway, for taking this book to
a whole new level; my parents Ron and Helen;
my parents-in-law Bruce and Cynthya; my two
amazing aunties, Aunty Carol and Aunty Fay, who
have always been there for me; my big brother Mick
and his family Leanne, Ben, Jade and Mitchell;
my brother Ian and his family Nikki, Georgia and
Jack; my sister Kazz and her family Adrian, Zack,
Ivy, Charlie and Ella; David Thorold, my 'Uncle D'
in New Guinea; my cousins Mary-Anne, Ollie, Ron
and Sophia, and their families.

Lastly, to my mates who I grew up with and who
have had a massive influence on my life: David Rixon,

thank you for your loyalty, wisdom, great sense of humour and organising the group catch-ups, you are a one-in-a-million friend; David Fordham, your strength and determination in facing the countless surgeries and rehab for your recent injuries is truly inspirational; Nathan 'Super-Ted' Fordham, thank you for being a role model for strength by never succumbing to the group who were constantly trying to make you change your mind about everything from fashion to lifestyle choices; Trent Fordham, your attention to detail and unique ability to accurately sum up a situation/person in a single, amusing sentence is a testament to your genius; and Shawn 'Stress' Chard, you are the most laid-back person I know, a gentle giant with serious brains and a freakish strength which could have seen you be a powerlifter.

Dr Anthony Gunn is a psychologist
and internationally published
author. He regularly helps people
to step out of their comfort zone.
Anthony and his wife, Melissa, are
the parents of two children.

Anthony's publications include:
Get Happy: Lessons in lasting happiness
Swing High: Life lessons from childhood
Walk Tall: 100 ways to live life to the fullest
*Raising Confident Happy Children: 40 Tips for helping
your child succeed.*

For more info go to: www.AnthonyGunn.com